Mohammed Reza Pahlavi

Linda Barth

CHELSEA HOUSE
PUBLISHERS
A Haights Cross Communications Company

Philadelphia

CHELSEA HOUSE PUBLISHERS

EDITOR IN CHIEF Sally Cheney
DIRECTOR OF PRODUCTION Kim Shinners
CREATIVE MANAGER Takeshi Takahashi
MANUFACTURING MANAGER Diann Grasse

Staff for MOHAMMED REZA PAHLAVI

EDITOR Lee Marcott
ASSOCIATE EDITOR Bill Conn
PRODUCTION ASSISTANT Jaimie Winkler
PICTURE RESEARCH 21st Century Publishing and Communications, Inc.
SERIES AND COVER DESIGNER Takeshi Takahashi
LAYOUT 21st Century Publishing and Communications, Inc.

A Haights Cross Communications ◆— Company

http://www.chelseahouse.com

First Printing

1 3 5 7 9 8 6 4 2

Library of Congress Cataloging-in-Publication Data

Barth, Linda.
   Mohammed Reza Pahlavi / Linda Barth.
      p. cm.—(Major world leaders)
Summary: Provides an overview of the history of Iran and describes the life and times of
Mohammed Reza Pahlavi, the former Shah of Iran. Includes bibliographical references
and index.
   ISBN 0-7910-6948-6
   1. Mohammed Reza Pahlavi, Shah of Iran, 1919– —Juvenile literature. 2. Iran—Kings
and rulers—Biography—Juvenile literature. [1. Mohammed Reza Pahlavi, Shah of Iran,
1919– 2. Kings, queens, rulers, etc. 3. Iran—History.] I. Title. II. Series.
DS318.M65 B37 2002
955.05'3'092—dc21

                                                                          20020075130

TABLE OF CONTENTS

On Leadership

Arthur M. Schlesinger, jr.

Leadership, it may be said, is really what makes the world go round. Love no doubt smoothes the passage; but love is a private transaction between consenting adults. Leadership is a public transaction with history. The idea of leadership affirms the capacity of individuals to move, inspire, and mobilize masses of people so that they act together in pursuit of an end. Sometimes leadership serves good purposes, sometimes bad; but whether the end is benign or evil, great leaders are those men and women who leave their personal stamp on history.

Now, the very concept of leadership implies the proposition that individuals can make a difference. This proposition has never been universally accepted. From classical times to the present day, eminent thinkers have regarded individuals as no more than the agents and pawns of larger forces, whether the gods and goddesses of the ancient world or, in the modern era, race, class, nation, the dialectic, the will of the people, the spirit of the times, history itself. Against such forces, the individual dwindles into insignificance.

So contends the thesis of historical determinism. Tolstoy's great novel *War and Peace* offers a famous statement of the case. Why, Tolstoy asked, did millions of men in the Napoleonic Wars, denying their human feelings and their common sense, move back and forth across Europe slaughtering their fellows? "The war," Tolstoy answered, "was bound to happen simply because it was bound to happen." All prior history determined it. As for leaders, they, Tolstoy said, "are but the labels that serve to give a name to an end and, like labels, they have the least possible connection with the event." The greater the leader, "the more conspicuous the inevitability and the predestination of every act he commits." The leader, said Tolstoy, is "the slave of history."

Determinism takes many forms. Marxism is the determinism of class. Nazism the determinism of race. But the idea of men and women as the slaves of history runs athwart the deepest human instincts. Rigid determinism abolishes the idea of human freedom—the assumption of free choice that underlies every move we make, every word we speak, every thought we think. It abolishes the idea of human responsibility, since it is manifestly unfair to reward or punish people for actions that are by definition beyond their control. No one can live consistently by any deterministic creed. The Marxist states prove this themselves by their extreme susceptibility to the cult of leadership.

More than that, history refutes the idea that individuals make no difference. In December 1931 a British politician crossing Fifth Avenue in New York City between 76th and 77th Streets around 10:30 P.M. looked in the wrong direction and was knocked down by an automobile— a moment, he later recalled, of a man aghast, a world aglare: "I do not understand why I was not broken like an eggshell or squashed like a gooseberry." Fourteen months later an American politician, sitting in an open car in Miami, Florida, was fired on by an assassin; the man beside him was hit. Those who believe that individuals make no difference to history might well ponder whether the next two decades would have been the same had Mario Constasino's car killed Winston Churchill in 1931 and Giuseppe Zangara's bullet killed Franklin Roosevelt in 1933. Suppose, in addition, that Lenin had died of typhus in Siberia in 1895 and that Hitler had been killed on the western front in 1916. What would the 20th century have looked like now?

For better or for worse, individuals do make a difference. "The notion that a people can run itself and its affairs anonymously," wrote the philosopher William James, "is now well known to be the silliest of absurdities. Mankind does nothing save through initiatives on the part of inventors, great or small, and imitation by the rest of us—these are the sole factors in human progress. Individuals of genius show the way, and set the patterns, which common people then adopt and follow."

Leadership, James suggests, means leadership in thought as well as in action. In the long run, leaders in thought may well make the greater difference to the world. "The ideas of economists and political philosophers, both when they are right and when they are wrong," wrote John Maynard Keynes, "are more powerful than is commonly understood. Indeed the world is ruled by little else. Practical men, who believe themselves to be quite exempt from any intellectual influences, are usually the slaves of some defunct economist. . . . The power of vested interests is vastly exaggerated compared with the gradual encroachment of ideas."

But, as Woodrow Wilson once said, "Those only are leaders of men, in the general eye, who lead in action. . . . It is at their hands that new thought gets its translation into the crude language of deeds." Leaders in thought often invent in solitude and obscurity, leaving to later generations the tasks of imitation. Leaders in action—the leaders portrayed in this series—have to be effective in their own time.

And they cannot be effective by themselves. They must act in response to the rhythms of their age. Their genius must be adapted, in a phrase from William James, "to the receptivities of the moment." Leaders are useless without followers. "There goes the mob," said the French politician, hearing a clamor in the streets. "I am their leader. I must follow them." Great leaders turn the inchoate emotions of the mob to purposes of their own. They seize on the opportunities of their time, the hopes, fears, frustrations, crises, potentialities. They succeed when events have prepared the way for them, when the community is awaiting to be aroused, when they can provide the clarifying and organizing ideas. Leadership completes the circuit between the individual and the mass and thereby alters history.

It may alter history for better or for worse. Leaders have been responsible for the most extravagant follies and most monstrous crimes that have beset suffering humanity. They have also been vital in such gains as humanity has made in individual freedom, religious and racial tolerance, social justice, and respect for human rights.

There is no sure way to tell in advance who is going to lead for good and who for evil. But a glance at the gallery of men and women in MAJOR WORLD LEADERS suggests some useful tests.

One test is this: Do leaders lead by force or by persuasion? By command or by consent? Through most of history leadership was exercised by the divine right of authority. The duty of followers was to defer and to obey. "Theirs not to reason why/Theirs but to do and die." On occasion, as with the so-called enlightened despots of the 18th century in Europe, absolutist leadership was animated by humane purposes. More often, absolutism nourished the passion for domination, land, gold, and conquest and resulted in tyranny.

The great revolution of modern times has been the revolution of equality. "Perhaps no form of government," wrote the British historian James Bryce in his study of the United States, *The American Commonwealth*, "needs great leaders so much as democracy." The idea that all people should be equal in their legal condition has undermined the old structure of authority, hierarchy, and deference. The revolution of equality has had two contrary effects on the nature of leadership. For equality, as Alexis de Tocqueville pointed out in his great study *Democracy in America*, might mean equality in servitude as well as equality in freedom.

"I know of only two methods of establishing equality in the political world," Tocqueville wrote. "Rights must be given to every citizen, or none at all to anyone . . . save one, who is the master of all." There was no middle ground "between the sovereignty of all and the absolute power of one man." In his astonishing prediction of 20th-century totalitarian dictatorship, Tocqueville explained how the revolution of equality could lead to the *Führerprinzip* and more terrible absolutism than the world had ever known.

But when rights are given to every citizen and the sovereignty of all is established, the problem of leadership takes a new form, becomes more exacting than ever before. It is easy to issue commands and enforce them by the rope and the stake, the concentration camp and the *gulag*. It is much harder to use argument and achievement to overcome opposition and win consent. The Founding Fathers of the United States understood the difficulty. They believed that history had given them the opportunity to decide, as Alexander Hamilton wrote in the first Federalist Paper, whether men are indeed capable of basing government on "reflection and choice, or whether they are forever destined to depend . . . on accident and force."

Government by reflection and choice called for a new style of leadership and a new quality of followership. It required leaders to be responsive to popular concerns, and it required followers to be active and informed participants in the process. Democracy does not eliminate emotion from politics; sometimes it fosters demagoguery; but it is confident that, as the greatest of democratic leaders put it, you cannot fool all of the people all of the time. It measures leadership by results and retires those who overreach or falter or fail.

It is true that in the long run despots are measured by results too. But they can postpone the day of judgment, sometimes indefinitely, and in the meantime they can do infinite harm. It is also true that democracy is no guarantee of virtue and intelligence in government, for the voice of the people is not necessarily the voice of God. But democracy, by assuring the right of opposition, offers built-in resistance to the evils inherent in absolutism. As the theologian Reinhold Niebuhr summed it up, "Man's capacity for justice makes democracy possible, but man's inclination to justice makes democracy necessary."

A second test for leadership is the end for which power is sought. When leaders have as their goal the supremacy of a master race or the promotion of totalitarian revolution or the acquisition and exploitation of colonies or the protection of greed and privilege or the preservation of personal power, it is likely that their leadership will do little to advance the cause of humanity. When their goal is the abolition of slavery, the liberation of women, the enlargement of opportunity for the poor and powerless, the extension of equal rights to racial minorities, the defense of the freedoms of expression and opposition, it is likely that their leadership will increase the sum of human liberty and welfare.

Leaders have done great harm to the world. They have also conferred great benefits. You will find both sorts in this series. Even "good" leaders must be regarded with a certain wariness. Leaders are not demigods; they put on their trousers one leg after another just like ordinary mortals. No leader is infallible, and every leader needs to be reminded of this at regular intervals. Irreverence irritates leaders but is their salvation. Unquestioning submission corrupts leaders and demeans followers. Making a cult of a leader is always a mistake. Fortunately hero worship generates its own antidote. "Every hero," said Emerson, "becomes a bore at last."

The signal benefit the great leaders confer is to embolden the rest of us to live according to our own best selves, to be active, insistent, and resolute in affirming our own sense of things. For great leaders attest to the reality of human freedom against the supposed inevitabilities of history. And they attest to the wisdom and power that may lie within the most unlikely of us, which is why Abraham Lincoln remains the supreme example of great leadership. A great leader, said Emerson, exhibits new possibilities to all humanity. "We feed on genius . . . . Great men exist that there may be greater men."

Great leaders, in short, justify themselves by emancipating and empowering their followers. So humanity struggles to master its destiny, remembering with Alexis de Tocqueville: "It is true that around every man a fatal circle is traced beyond which he cannot pass; but within the wide verge of that circle he is powerful and free; as it is with man, so with communities." ■

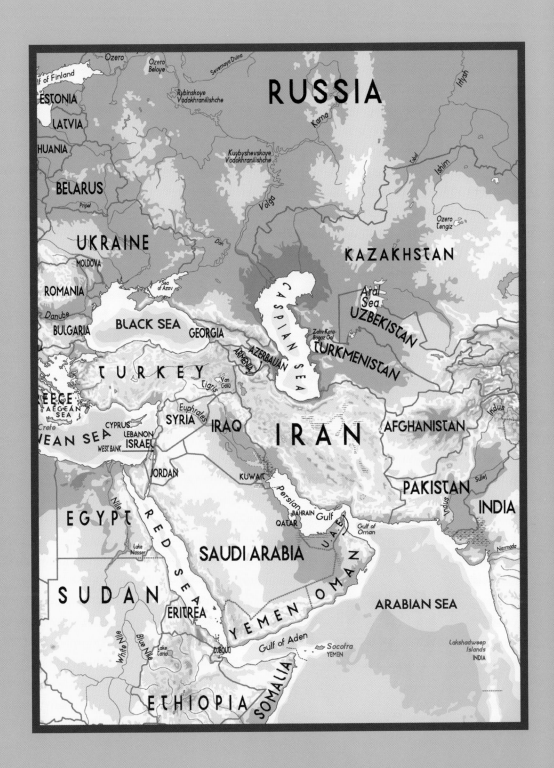

An Iranian soldier shows his devotion by kneeling in front of Shah Mohammed Reza Pahlavi as Empress Farah, the shah's wife, looks on.

1

The Shah and His Country

I t was a quiet afternoon in January 1979 at the airport in Tehran, the capital of Iran. Instead of his usual entourage, Shah Mohammed Reza Pahlavi, the ruler of Iran, had arrived with his wife, his doctor, and his two dogs. The shah, or king, had bid farewell to his few close friends still in the country. Now, as he boarded a private jet, he assured himself that he would be returning soon enough. But he didn't know if he was seeing his country for the last time, or if the tide of revolution that had washed across his nation might still be stopped. Either way, it was a painful departure for a man who considered himself the physical embodiment of his country.

He could not have known that once outside of Iran he would be treated as an international pariah, abandoned by his allies and pitied by his friends. Frail, sick with cancer, and seemingly unable to understand the fate that had befallen him, the shah had become a man without a home. He had once ruled of the most powerful country in the Middle East, a country once courted by the both the United States and the Soviet Union.

The rise and fall of Shah Mohammed Reza Pahlavi is one of the most dramatic political stories in modern history. Iran is one of the largest countries in the Middle East, and it has always been a country of vast contradictions. It is a land rich with oil where much of the population lives in abject poverty. Mohammed Reza was the second and last shah in the Pahlavi dynasty. Under his rule Iran was convulsed by the Cold War, the oil boom, and the rise of Islamic fundamentalism. To understand Mohammed Reza's life, it is important to understand the land he ruled. He believed that God had chosen him to rule his people and that he was, literally, the soul of Iran.

What is now called Iran was once known as Persia. The name was changed to Iran after World War II, and Iranians are still referred to as Persians. (To simplify the descriptions in this book, the country will always be referred to as Iran.) Unlike their neighbors in the Middle East, they are not Arabs—they speak Farsi rather than Arabic. The Persian Empire was founded by Cyrus the Great in 546 B.C., and his domain covered nearly all of what is now the Middle East. From the beginning, the area was a vital strategic link between East and West, a bridge between Asia and Europe. Modern day Iran's neighbors include Iraq, Afghanistan, Bahrain, and Russia. From the time of Cyrus onward, power in Iran would change hands frequently, as empires rose and fell around it.

In 330 B.C., Iran was conquered by Alexander the Great. He controlled one of the greatest empires of all time, stretching from Asia to Europe. While he was a benevolent ruler, his death led to decades of savage struggle for control of the Greek Empire. Two tribes, the Parthians and the Sassanians, dominated Iran until the seventh century A.D., when Muslim Arabs invading from the east took over.

The history of modern Iran is intertwined with the history

This engraving depicts the prophet Muhammad, the founder of Islam. Muslims believe that Muhammad is the messenger of God.

of Islam. The religion dates to the birth of Muhammad in 570 A.D. Muslims believe that Muhammad is the messenger of God, or Allah. As a young man, Muhammad began having visions, messages from Allah that came to be embodied in the Koran, the Muslim bible. These laws, sent from Allah to his people through Muhammad, became the basis for Islam. From the beginning, Islam was more than just a religion, it was a political movement; the Koran contains as many practical laws as it does spiritual. The response to Muhammad's preaching was astounding. Within a hundred years, Islam had spread from Muhammad's homeland of Saudi Arabia across the Middle East, as far west as Spain and as far east as India.

One of the many lessons of Islam was that the rule of the mullahs, or holy teachers, should always come before the rule of kings. The hope was that this would protect Muslims from harsh rulers. In Iran it meant that the mullahs were a buffer between the people and the shahs. Even then, it was important for the shahs to maintain an open and friendly relationship with religious leaders. The mullahs looked to the shahs for financial support, and the shahs relied on the mullahs to keep their subjects happy. It was always a tense relationship, and as Mohammed Reza would learn the hard way, one that was not to be taken lightly.

The rise of Islam in Iran did not prevent foreign powers from taking an interest in its location and its resources. It was a major trade route between Europe and Asia, and Iran grew wealthy. In 1219, Mongol hordes under Genghis Khan began arriving in Iran, on their way west. In 1380, Tamerlane, a Mongol warrior whose empire stretched from India to the Mediterranean, began to move into Iran from the east. The area was soon under his control, and his presence brought about a resurgence of wealth and culture. But no one, including Tamerlane, could keep control of Iran for long. Early in the 16th century a number of smaller, local dynasties emerged throughout the area, which was dominated by fierce tribes that vied for power.

In the mid-1700s, Afghanistan invaded Iran, only to be promptly overthrown. The Iranian army, not content to simply toss the Afghans out, marched straight through Afghanistan and took control of India. It was the first sign that modern Iran was a powerful nation. At the end of the 18th century, Zand rulers, dominant in the south, were replaced by the Qajars, a Turkish tribe. (Turkey's influence at the time stretched from Eastern

Thamas Koulikan, also known as Nadir Shah, ruled Iran from 1736 to 1747. He became ruler after winning battles against invading forces of Afghans and Turks.

Europe across the Middle East.) Still, that did not stop the British from moving into Iran in the middle of the 19th century.

Because Iran was a safe route to India, by then a major part of the British Empire, the British wanted to preserve its independence, if not control it outright. Russia, under the rule of the czars (kings), had emerged as a world power by this time. Russia had its own interest in Iran, since the two countries shared a border. Great Britain and Russia would struggle for control over Iran for the next century, while the shahs grew even wealthier by playing the two countries against each other. Iran was a buffer between the two empires, and they each had a sphere of influence, with the British dominating the south while the Russians put pressure on the north (along their mutual border). But as the British and the Russians bickered over trade routes and tariffs, neither could have predicted the course Iran's future was to take because of a resource that had not yet been discovered. Oil would change everything.

Oil is used to fuel cars, heat buildings, and to make a variety of products, including plastics. The United States, like many other Western nations, does not have nearly oil enough to meet the demand and must rely on oil-rich nations like Iran for supplies. Oil forms underground, and scientists and geologists work together to determine where it exists. It is removed by oil wells, which dig deep below the earth and pump the oil up into containers. Then it is refined, meaning impurities are removed, and it is put into barrels for sale. When oil was discovered in Iran and many other Middle Eastern countries in the late 19th and early 20th centuries, those countries lacked the resources to develop oil wells and to sell the product abroad. Very often, a country like Iran would sell what is called a concession, which allowed another nation or even a private company to pay a certain amount of money for the right to extract and sell oil.

Iran's major oil deposits were in the south, and in 1901 Iran gave complete control of its oil to a British entrepreneur named William Knox D'Arcy. D'Arcy controlled oil exploration and extraction for 480,000 square miles and was required to pay Shah Mozaf al-Din a mere 16 percent of his profit. The British government quickly realized how much money was to be made and bought the contract from D'Arcy in 1909. By 1932 the British would sell 6.5 million tons of Iranian oil a year, earning enormous profits. Iran, in comparison, earned next to nothing. Meanwhile, the Russians worried as the balance of power tilted toward the

British. That changed with the coming of World War I.

The history of Iran provides an excellent example of how a major event in one country can have enormous repercussions around the world. During World War I, the Ottoman Empire collapsed. The Ottoman Empire was all that remained of the Turkish power that had once dominated the region. The Middle East fell under the influence of the Western Allies, which included Britain, France, Russia, and the United States. At the same time, Russia was recovering from its revolution, in which its monarchy had been overthrown by Communists. All of this would have an impact on Iran in the 1920s.

First, the new Russian regime wanted to exert more control over Iran. Now that the Communists were in charge, they were more concerned about protecting their borders than the czars had been, and their relationship to the British had become more openly hostile. Second, the new Russian government was angered by what it saw as British greed. The average Iranian was desperately poor and uneducated. Meanwhile, Britain was getting rich from Iran's natural resources. Russia declared all of its treaties with Britain null and void, meaning that their agreements not to fight over Iran were no longer valid. Russia began encouraging Iranians to resist British domination, in part by refusing to renew British oil agreements. Between 1918 and 1921, the British and the Russians played a cat and mouse game with Iran as the prize. In the meantime, the Iranian economy grew weaker and its people grew more and more disillusioned with their leaders. Although Iran had a constitutional monarchy, meaning that it had both a king and a democratically elected parliament called the Majlis, there was a great deal of corruption and the average Iranian had little say in how the country was run. British troops in the south and Russian troops in the north made Iran seem like a war zone. It was in the midst of this unrest that a young Russian-trained army commander named Reza Khan rose to seize power.

Reza Shah Pahlavi was the ruler of Iran from 1925 to 1941, during which time he stressed Iran's modernization and independence from foreign influence.

2

Rise of the Pahlavi Dynasty

The man who would come to call himself Reza Shah Pahlavi was a tall, handsome man with a strong voice and a deep sense of purpose. He was the commander of the Cossack Brigade, a Russian-funded force that was the only organized militia in Iran. With a show of his military might, he declared himself commander in chief of Iran's armed forces.

Under a 1906 constitution that was written by the ruling Qajars, with the help of the British, the Majlis was established as the Iranian Parliament. The people of Iran elected the leaders, and they helped balance the power of the shah. Once Reza declared himself shah in 1925, he essentially removed the power of the Majlis. He then set about ruthlessly bringing Iran's many tribal factions under the control of a central authority. His authority.

Historically, the countries of the Middle East had remained

divided by tribal loyalties, making them difficult to rule and therefore difficult to modernize. The modern borders of these nations had been drawn by the British and French at the end of World War I, with little regard for ethnic and religious differences. The 1920s saw the rise of a new form of nationalism. Young men who had grown up watching foreigners become wealthy from their country's resources decided it was time for their people to benefit. Reza Shah wanted Iran to be a truly independent nation, free of the influence of both the British and the Russians. Although he had been trained by the Russians, many saw him as an agent of the British—some would later claim that the British had helped him take the throne. But primarily he was interested in the well being of Iran. He came to power in 1925, at a time when Iranians were feeling frustrated by their standard of living and by the lack of attention from their leaders in Tehran. Reza Shah wanted to change that. He saw that Iran was making other nations rich while its own people were suffering, and he was determined to gain control of his country's oil fields. He was a strong and blunt leader, and he led Iran out of its role as pawn between superpowers. He expanded his country's role in regional politics and made strong allies with neighbors like Syria, Egypt, and the Soviet Union. His attempts at diplomacy, and his insistence that Iran be seen as more than simply a source of cash for Western countries, gave Iran a new form of independence. It was this independent streak that would eventually lead to his downfall.

One of the most important aspects of Reza Shah's reign was his insistence on modernizing Iran. He built roads and schools, and sent students abroad to learn skills like engineering. He was determined to bring his country into the 20th century. He frequently overrode, or even ignored, the advice of the clergy, which had encouraged him to become shah. He saw the influence of the mullah's as being old-fashioned and of holding back the development of a modern society in Iran. The mullahs had played a major role in Iranian politics and daily life since the arrival of Islam in the seventh century, but Reza Shah was not interested in appeasing them as his predecessors had done. At the time, many in Iran were open to the idea of leaving traditional religious rule behind. The clergy had grown wealthy, and the shah seized their lands (becoming by far the largest landholder in Iran in the process).

Strict adherence to Islam forbids women from appearing in public and demands that its followers closely obey the laws of the Koran. Reza Shah thought that if Iran was to compete for a place in the world, it would need to leave such traditions behind. But he was not diplomatic when it came to dealing with the mullahs and the ayatollahs, Iranian religious leaders. He banned many of their rites, and in one instance he publicly whipped an ayatollah for disobeying his command. To some degree, the suppression of religious leaders and their influence over daily life was embraced in Iran. Reza Shah was a strong and respected leader, and under his rule, Iranians saw their standard of living increase. He told them that Iran was an important country and that it should be respected by the world. This sort of nationalism appealed to the people. It offered them hope of a better station in life. By the time his son, Shah Mohammed Reza Pahlavi, had been in power for two decades, that attitude would have sharply changed.

But first Reza Shah had to become shah. Ironically, he achieved that status thanks to the British government. As had happened in the past, the problems of other countries would be played out at the expense of Iran's stability. In the late 1930s, Nazi Germany was already beginning to advance on territory in the Middle East and Northern Africa. The Nazi leader, Adolf Hitler, had already made it clear that his goal was world domination, and the countries that would later help make up the Allied forces in World War II—Britain, France, the United States, and Russia—were understandably nervous about the German presence in Iran. The Russians and British were particularly concerned because a German invasion

Reza Shah is shown on the Peacock Throne in 1931. The throne is solid gold inlaid with precious stones.

of the Middle East threatened both their empires and their economies. The British still ruled over much of southeast Asia, including India; and the Soviets controlled many of Iran's neighbors. Russia and Britain both profited from the oil trade, and if Germany invaded Iran, oil supplies would be threatened. Also, Russia and Britain knew that when they entered the war against Germany, they would have trouble supplying oil to their armies if Germany controlled Middle Eastern oil supplies.

At the beginning of the war, Reza Shah had welcomed

Germans into Iran in his bid to achieve independence from the British and the Soviets. It was an error in judgment that would eventually cost him the throne. Although he declared that Iran would remain neutral, the world believed he was sympathetic to Hitler's cause. Hitler had courted the shah's favor by telling him that he believed Iranians were members of the Aryan race, which Hitler defined as a supposedly superior race of white people. Unlike their Arab neighbors, whom Hitler regarded an inferior race, Iranians would have a place in Hitler's new world order. When the Germans invaded Russia and began bombing Britain, the shah's neutrality began to look more and more like support. While his reasons for supporting Germany may have had little to do with the Nazi racial philosophy, it made no difference. By 1941 the British and Soviets were both at war with Germany, and Iran's neutrality had become a serious issue. It was a strategic strong point, and Hitler saw that either conquering Iran or signing it on as an ally was the key to toppling the British Empire since it would provide easy access to India, which was still under British protection. The loss of Iran to Germany would allow the Nazis easy ground access to Asia and help advance their plan for a world takeover. The Soviets feared that a German presence in Iran would make it easy for Hitler to invade Russia from the south.

In July 1941 the British and Russians asked Reza Shah to expel all German agents from Iran and to deny German influence. For reasons that have never been clear, he hesitated, which was a fatal error. The Russians and the British invaded Iran. The Soviets sent troops into Iran on the grounds that they needed to protect their borders. The British, in turn, sent troops both to protect their interests in India and to guard against a Soviet takeover of Iran. Once again, the country was entangled in conflict over foreign interests.

Britain's prime minister, Winston Churchill, warned the shah and his government about the possibility of a Soviet takeover after the war. He said that unless the British had free reign to control Iran, the Soviets would eventually take control of the capital. Churchill persuaded the government in Tehran to believe that without British forces to counterbalance the Soviet influence, Iran would end up occupied by Russia at the end of the war. The pressure on Reza Shah was too great for him to bear. He was asked to choose between answering to the British or being conquered by the Soviets. Unable to live under the domination of the British, and faced with a complete loss of control, he abdicated the throne in 1941. He told his son Mohammed Reza, "I cannot be the nominal head of an occupied land, to be dictated to by some minor English or Russian officer." He was exiled to South Africa, where he died in 1944.

The British had to keep control of Iran and that meant installing a new shah who would answer to them unconditionally. Otherwise, Iranians might feel they had been conquered and rebel against the British. But Britain needed a leader it could control. Mohammed Reza had been his father's choice to ascend the throne upon his death. He was the eldest son of the shah's 11 children, and he and his twin sister Ashraf were born on October 26, 1919. When Reza Shah made himself ruler and established the Pahlavi dynasty, he had named Mohammed Reza the crown prince. He had been raised amid the wealth and isolation of royalty, spoiled by his mother and twin sister, with whom he had an especially close relationship all his life. He was schooled in Europe and lived a life of privilege that most Iranians could scarcely imagine. By the time his father abdicated the throne, Mohammed Reza had done little with his life and was considered a playboy. His attitude toward Germany was unclear, but he seemed to sympathize with the Nazis the way his father had.

The British considered several options, including reinstalling the royal family, the Qajars, that Reza Shah had overthrown. In the end, the British selected Mohammed Reza because they believed he would be easy to manipulate and control. To a degree, they were correct, but in time the very weakness that had seemed so appealing would come to cost the West dearly.

As a young man, Mohammed Reza was groomed by his father to become the next ruler of Iran and continue the Pahlavi dynasty. Shah Reza did not know that his son was to be the last Iranian shah.

And for many in Iran, Mohammed Reza's decision to take the throne his father had been forced from was an unforgivable betrayal. In their eyes it made him a puppet of the West, a false leader who answered to foreign governments. From the start, the new shah was the cause of dissent.

The future shah attended school in Europe and adopted a Western style of dress. He believed that he had been chosen by Allah to lead Iran.

3

Shah Mohammed Reza Pahlavi

Shah Mohammed Reza Pahlavi was not the same kind of man or ruler that his father had been. He had been a quiet and shy boy who was carefully watched by his mother and twin sister Ashraf. When he was seven, he nearly died of typhoid. During a high fever, he had a vision in which Ali, the son-in-law of the prophet Muhammad, came to him. In Shi'ite Islam, the religion of Iran, Ali is considered second in importance only to Muhammad himself. (The majority of Muslims are Sunni, having followed several of Muhammad's advisers rather than Ali after the prophet's death.) He began to recover the day after his vision, and he would frequently tell the story as an illustration of his belief that he had been chosen by Allah himself to lead Iran.

Despite his belief in divine protection, he was a self-doubting boy who lived in fear of his tyrannical father. His twin sister Ashraf was brash and outspoken, but because she was a girl, she was forbidden to inherit the throne. Still, when her father was exiled and she prepared to leave Iran with him, he told her to stay, insisting that her brother needed her more than he did. Reza Shah seemed to recognize that his son was weak-willed, and that he would need the help and protection of his iron-willed sister. Princess Ashraf always said that her father essentially ignored her because, as a girl, she had no political future. He had no way of knowing that she would come to serve as her brother's adviser and that her role in the royal family would help bring about its downfall.

Reza Shah had had little formal education, but he was determined that his son receive a good education. He sent Mohammed Reza to a Swiss boarding school, Le Rosey, where he studied alongside the children of some of the wealthiest and most powerful families in the world. He would later say that his years in Switzerland had been the most important of his life because it was where he learned about democracy. Given that his country was ruled by a monarchy, such a thing might seem strange, but it was only one of many of the contradictions by which the future shah lived his life. "I believe in democracy," he would later say, "but not without discipline." Perhaps that is why he maintained a parliament, but made sure that he always had the final say.

Mohammed Reza returned from Switzerland at age 17, in 1937. When he had left for school five years earlier, Tehran was still in many ways a city of the past, with no electricity and dusty unpaved roads. By the time he returned, his father had revolutionized the capital, installing broad, paved avenues in place of winding streets, and bringing electricity to the city. It was beginning to resemble a Western city for the first time in its history. The young crown prince quickly became a staple of Tehran's social scene—which earned him his reputation among the British as a playboy. His father asked little of him, and he enrolled in an officer training program where he learned to fly

Princess Fawzia of Egypt was chosen to become the wife of Mohammed Reza. The couple is shown here on their wedding day with members of the royal families in attendance.

planes. He loved being a pilot, and it was a hobby he would indulge for the rest of his life.

When he was 19 years old, Mohammed Reza's father decided that it was time for him to marry. A crown prince must have a carefully chosen wife, so his father began to travel throughout the Middle East, searching for the right bride. Not only did she have to be of royal descent, but she had to be from a family of strategic significance. Reza Shah was not romantic. He thought his son's marriage should help forge an alliance, not necessarily be a love match. As it turned out, the woman he selected for his son was renowned as a great beauty. Princess Fawzia of Egypt, the favorite sister of Egyptian King Farouk I became Mohammed Reza's wife in the spring of 1939. She was 17 years old.

In 1940, Princess Shahnaz was born. Because she was a girl, and therefore could not be heir to the throne, she was something of a disappointment to her father and grandfather. By then, the marriage had begun to falter. Princess Fawzia was used to the cosmopolitan, cultured life of the Cairo court. Living in Tehran, a city that was a backwater by comparison, was like being sent into exile. Mohammed Reza's unfaithfulness contributed to the marriage ending by the time World War II reached Iran.

Mohammed Reza did not have much time to dwell on the failure of his first marriage. He was barely 22 when he ascended the throne, and he knew that he was seen by many as nothing more than an Anglo-Soviet puppet. He was furious that the British and the Russians once again seemed to be dictating Iran's future. Now that he was shah, he decided he needed help to escape the control of the two governments that had disgraced his father. By 1944, American troops had entered Tehran. The shah realized that the Americans acted apart from both the British and the Russians. They maintained their own independence, and the shah saw in them hope for Iran's future. He was correct, and his appeal for help to the United States did not go unanswered.

Although the war would not end until 1945, the Allies were confident of their victory. The U.S. president, Franklin Delano Roosevelt, was already concerned with the influence Britain and Russia would seek to exert after the war. He worried that, with their troops already on the ground in places like Iran, they would take advantage of the war's end by expanding their power, if not their empires. Roosevelt felt that the United States should discourage this and help struggling nations maintain their independence. If possible, the United States should help build them into modern, Western-style democracies. When he heard about the shah's appeal, he saw Iran as a prime candidate for such a transformation. In a memo to his secretary of state, Cordell Hull, whose job was to handle such matters, Roosevelt wrote that he was, "thrilled by the idea of using Iran as an example of what we could do by an unselfish American policy. We could not take on a more difficult nation than Iran. I should like, however, to have a try at it."

President Roosevelt saw Iran as a "difficult nation" for several reasons. First, despite the attempts by Mohammed Reza's father to modernize his country, Iran was still poor. Most of its people were illiterate, and there was little in the way of health care or schooling, even for the wealthiest Iranians. In fact, when Mohammed Reza was sick with typhoid, the royal family had to scour Tehran looking for medicine. Second, although the shah's father had united the country, there were still the mullahs to contend with, and Islam was still a powerful religious and political force, especially among the poor. Third, and perhaps most importantly, the Russians and the British were not about to let a geographic prize like Iran slip from their hands without a fight. After all, the land was not only strategically located, but it was loaded with oil. Iran's oil reserves had barely been tapped, and already they were worth a fortune. In a postwar world, with new developments in technology, the opportunities were endless.

Roosevelt pressured Churchill, who finally conceded to pulling his troops out of Iran after the war. The Russians agreed, too, but after the war they set up puppet states in neighboring Azerbaijan and Kurdistan. The young shah refused to be bullied by the Russians and turned to the newly founded United Nations for help. Harry Truman, who had taken over the presidency after Roosevelt's death, threatened the Russians, with whom he was also struggling over control of Eastern Europe. The Cold War, the nonviolent feud between the United States and the Soviet Union, had begun almost immediately after World War II ended. Yet again, Iran was like a chess piece in a game being played by two major world powers. This time the Russians backed down, and Mohammed Reza took their withdrawal from the Iranian border as a clear sign of both America's strength and its friendship. When the

President Harry Truman (left) attended a dinner in Washington with the shah is 1949. The leaders were allied against Russia during much of the Cold War.

separatist Tudeh (People's) Party attempted to take control of Azerbaijan and Kurdistan, two of Iran's northernmost provinces, the shah sent troops to crush the rebellion. The prime minister, Ahmed Qavam, oversaw the action and most Iranians supported this move—they were fearful that Russia wanted Iran as a satellite state.

Russia had already extended its control over much of Eastern Europe, where Communist parties that answered to Moscow were in control of local governments. President Truman encouraged the shah to be wary of Soviet expansion, which Truman saw as a threat to democracy around the world. Mohammad Reza felt secure, knowing that America would help defend his country against the Soviet Union. That sense of security allowed him to begin truly leading his people.

It also allowed him the freedom to enjoy a personal life. By 1948 the shah had divorced Princess Fawzia and was enjoying the nightlife in the burgeoning city of Tehran. After the war, the United States had invested in Iran, as had the British, and the economy was in an upswing, thanks to the strong demand for oil. The shah spent much of his time in nightclubs, and in 1949 he married Soraya Esfandiari, an 18-year-old he had met while out on the town. This time the marriage was for love, and the fact that her mother was German helped cement the opinion in the rest of the world that the shah was a modern leader friendly to the West. But that same year, the unhappiness of many of his subjects was made clear when an attempt was made on the shah's life. The would-be assassin was apparently a member of the Tudeh Party, which was associated with both Communism and religious extremism. The shah declared martial law, the Tudeh party was officially banned, and many of its members were arrested. It was the first time that the shah used his power to quash his political enemies at home. It would not be the last.

A demonstrator in Tehran holds a sign that was torn down from AIOC headquarters. The Iranians resented the oil agreement that allowed the British to earn enormous profits from Iranian oil.

4

The
Cold War

While the world had been at war, new political forces had arisen in Iran. As mentioned earlier, the British had long dominated the oil trade in Iran. By the end of World War II, the Anglo-Iranian Oil Company (AIOC) had become a major source of trouble in Iran. It was established in the late 1890s, and the bulk of its profits went to the British. The company essentially paid the Iranian government a flat fee in return for the right to drill for oil wherever and whenever it chose. The amount of income Iran received had little to do with how much oil the British took, and year after year, the British made tremendous amounts of money while the standard of living in Iran remained low.

Britain's presence in the oil business also served as a symbol of Iran's status in the world. As long as another country controlled its oil, Iran would remain, in essence, a colony, and not the world power it longed to be. For the next decade, the subject of Iran's control of its oil would dominate the political scene. It was the first major test of the shah's power, and it would reveal the weaknesses that he would later pay for with his throne.

In June 1950, Mohammed Reza appointed General Ali Razmara as prime minister (normally, the prime minister was named by the Majlis, but in this case the shah overruled them). The shah's family profited greatly from the arrangement with AIOC, and he was content with the status quo. The shah was proving to be more concerned about maintaining his own power than about providing the country with a strong prime minister. He wanted someone who would not defy his orders, and Razmara, a loyal army commander, seemed to fit the job. But he was an ineffective leader, and he immediately found himself overwhelmed by the controversy over the status of the AIOC. There were frequent protest marches, and even the middle class in cosmopolitan Tehran had begun to favor nationalization. Tensions were so high that when Razmara was assassinated by an Islamic activist in February 1951, the opposition openly celebrated his death. There were rumors that the shah had grown concerned that Razmara might give in to the will of the people and that he had ordered Razmara's assassination. Whether it was true or not, the shah was getting deeper and deeper into political trouble.

By now, nationalization was the leading issue in Iranian politics, and that led to the rise of Mohammed Mossadeq. After Razmara's death, the shah allowed the Majlis to appoint the next prime minister—he hoped that would appease them. They named Mohammed Mossadeq to the position in March 1951, and he was wildly popular with Iranians.

Mossadeq was a descendent of the Qajar dynasty that Reza Shah had overthrown in 1925, and a major landowner. He was born in the 1880s and was trained as a lawyer. He had served in the government for years, but he opposed Reza Shah's rise to power and was exiled to northern Iran. Mossadeq was opposed

Prime Minister Mohammed Mossadeq opposed both
the shah and the presence of the British in Iran.

to any foreign influence in Iran, but he had a particular hatred
of the British. He was completely opposed to the AIOC, and
he viewed the British with contempt, considering them conde-
scending and greedy. In his opinion Mohammed Reza was a
useless puppet. The shah was jetting off to Switzerland for ski

vacations, while his people were barely getting by. The middle class viewed Mossadeq as an educated and articulate statesman; to the lower classes he was a charismatic nationalist who promised them a better life. He had the full support of his people, and he set about dismantling the AIOC. For a brief time, it seemed that Mossadeq might become the leader of a new and progressive Iran.

The shah had become isolated in his palace and sulked about his loss of power. Mossadeq's government left the Shah with little to do, except play practical jokes. He liked to scare his wife's friends, for example, by putting plastic insects in their laps while they were playing bridge. A memo written for the British and the Americans about the rise of Mossadeq described the shah as "well-meaning, naturally well disposed towards Britain and the U.S., aware of the Communist danger, but vacillating and weak."

Understandably, the West was alarmed by the turn of events in Iran. The shah had lost control to Mossadeq, and the shah's advisers secretly turned to the British and the Americans for help. It was not hard to convince the two countries that they needed to intervene. With prodding from Britain, the United States became convinced that Mossadeq was getting too close to the Tudeh Party. In the midst of the Cold War, any association with Communism was seen by the West as a threat. The United States considered the Tudeh Party a pawn of the Soviet Union. The shah was smart enough to realize that this association would work to his advantage, although he was too indecisive to do anything about it. Unlike his father, who had been so self-assured, this shah desperately craved both flattery and approval. It was a dangerous combination, but one that served him well in dealing with Mossadeq. He was courted by the British and the Americans, who convinced him to gather his closest advisers, including high ranking army officers, and enlist them in a plot masterminded by the Central Intelligence Agency (CIA). The shah, who wanted so badly to rule and to be beloved by both his people and the West, was happy to oblige.

The plan was for the shah to release two decrees, one dismissing Mossadeq from his job as the head of the elected government and the other appointing General Fazlollah Zahedi prime minister. Kim Roosevelt, the son of Franklin and the head of the CIA's Middle East operations, arrived in Tehran to offer encouragement to the shah. Once Zahedi was in power, CIA agents would pay young men recruited from Tehran's slums to demonstrate in the streets in support of the shah. That way it would appear that the dismissal of Mossadeq was simply the shah's acknowledgment of the will of the people. Still the shah hesitated, too scared to act even with the assurances of Kim Roosevelt.

Finally, on August 12, 1953, he issued the decree. There were problems at first. Mossadeq arrested the palace messenger that delivered the word of his ouster. His supporters took to the streets, chanting, "Yankee go home!" They correctly guessed that the shah had acted with the backing of the United States. The shah panicked and fled to Iraq and then to Italy. He and his wife had barely had time to pack, and the media delighted in reporting that the Pahlavis arrived in Italy with nothing to wear. The Americans were horrified. To them, fleeing was the ultimate act of cowardice, and they feared that Mossadeq would soon be completely in control of Iran. It was the first time the shah fled his homeland, but it would not be the last.

In this instance, though, he was able to return. Thanks to the efforts of the CIA, the tide gradually turned in favor of the shah, and Mossadeq's supporters were replaced in the streets by the shah's supporters. The CIA spent thousands of dollars to encourage poor Iranians to take to the streets in support of the shah. Mohammed Reza and his wife had been virtual prisoners at their hotel in Italy—they had not thought to pack money, and their assets were tied up in Iran. When a reporter got word to

Reporters take notes as the shah reads a telegram in Rome, where he had fled after rioters protested his dismissal of Mossadeq.

them on August 19, 1953, that Mossadeq had been overthrown, the shah's response was, "I knew they [Iranians] loved me." It was yet another sign that he was out of touch with his people. The United States had saved the shah, and he was far from beloved by his people.

Mossadeq was put on trial, sentenced to three years of house arrest, and spent the rest of his life on his estate in northern Iran under constant guard. He died in 1967. The incident had a number of repercussions for the shah. First, he believed that once again Allah had spared him, and his belief in divine protection grew stronger. Second, he realized that his family needed to keep money outside of Iran, so that if they were ever again forced to flee, they would not be destitute. He and his family began amassing personal fortunes, often through corruption and at the expense of Iranians. And finally, he came to view the United States as his friend and savior.

That did not mean that he stopped playing the United States and the Soviet Union against each other. Throughout the 1950s, he demanded the United States provide him with massive military aid. The shah wanted money, and whenever the United States, then under the leadership of Dwight D. Eisenhower, refused him something, he would threaten to turn to the Soviets instead. The Cold War was at its peak in the 1950s, and the shah took full advantage. Mohammed Reza was convinced that Iran was the most important strategic ally of the United States. He also was personally obsessed with weaponry, an obsession that increased dramatically after the Mossadeq affair. Eisenhower was frequently frustrated with the shah, and once commented that the shah considered himself "a military genius" who ran the risk of destroying his country's economy by pouring all of its money into its army. Eisenhower had led the Allied troops in Europe during World War II, and in 1958, when the shah was once again threatening to turn to the Soviets, his advisers pushed him to flatter the shah by praising his military leadership. Mohammed Reza was so pleased by Eisenhower's compliments that he backed down. It was just another example of the shah's style—he was highly responsive to flattery.

In the meantime, the shah was facing a personal crisis. Though by all accounts he was deeply in love with Queen Soraya, she was unable to bear children. He already had a daughter from his first marriage, but he needed a son to serve as his heir. His only full brother, Ali Reza, who was next in line for the throne, had been killed in a plane crash in 1954. In 1958 the shah announced he was divorcing Soraya. In 1959 he married Farah Diba, a 21-year-old student. It was the start of a new chapter in his life.

The shah married his third wife, Farah Diba, in 1959 in the hopes that she would provide him with an heir to the throne.

5

The White Revolution

I n 1960, following the Mossadeq affair, Shah Mohammed Reza Pahlavi was more determined than ever to modernize Iran's economy along Western lines. He would use any means to push Iran into his vision of the future. The shah believed that Iran was destined to be what he called *Tamaddon-e Bozorg,* a great civilization. He saw his nation as being foremost among its Middle East neighbors—Iran was the shining light that would lead them all to a place among the world's great powers. Iran would be as important as it was when it was called Persia and was ruled by Cyrus the Great. And oil would pay for his dream.

In the 1950s the shah had begun to assume a greater direction over the day-to-day running of the government. By 1960 the shah had built up Iran's military and had created a secret police force, SAVAK, which was loyal to him and notorious for its brutality. But the shah had failed to deal with fundamental social and economic problems. There was widespread discontent with his rule, and even though SAVAK was ruthless in its punishment of those who opposed the shah, more and more people were speaking out against him. Not surprisingly, the clergy led the way. In the meantime, in an effort to please the people and to weaken the opposition, the shah had created two new political parties. One party was supposed to represent the government and the other party represented the loyal opposition, but they were both controlled by the shah himself. Neither party would criticize him. When general elections were finally held in 1960 they were so blatantly rigged that even the shah felt obligated to denounce them.

In January 1961, John F. Kennedy became president of the United States. He was more liberal than Eisenhower had been, and he pressured the shah to institute social reforms in return for military support. Kennedy was never fond of the shah, whom he felt was too timid and too indecisive to be an effective leader. Worse still, at a meeting with Soviet leader Nikita Krushchev, Kennedy had been warned that Iran was on the brink of revolution. Krushchev told Kennedy that the shah's regime would soon collapse under the pressure of Communist-led groups like the now-underground Tudeh Party and that Iran would align itself with the Russians. Azerbaijan and Kurdistan had already become part of the Soviet Union. Krushchev stressed to Kennedy that Iran's collapse would not be the result of Soviet intervention. Krushchev feared that the world would blame the Soviet Union for Iran's slide into Communism, a fact might set the stage for another world war. Kennedy was upset. He ordered a report on Iran's stability and was told that "profound political and social change in one form or another is virtually inevitable." In other words, the shah was going to be overthrown unless something changed, fast.

Kennedy pushed the shah to change his regime. In the

The long-term political association between Iran and the United States continued with President John Kennedy. The two leaders are shown here after a conference at the White House in 1962.

spring of 1962, the shah visited Washington and asked the president for more military aid. Kennedy insisted that the shah needed to be more concerned with his regime than with his army. But Mohammed Reza could not let go of his obsession with weapons. He told Kennedy that he envisioned a "first-class army" that would help Iran become a "showcase" nation, an example of the positive influence of the West on developing nations. Kennedy was not pleased, particularly when the shah said that he was sure the president understood that to keep Iran out of the hands of Communists, he would need absolute power. "[I am] not by nature a dictator. But if Iran is to succeed, its government [will] have to act firmly for a time." In other words, the shah said that he expected, "the U.S. would not insist that Iran do everything in an absolutely legal way." For example, the shah hoped to convince the United States to send home Iranian students his secret police considered Communists. There, they would be put on trial for their political beliefs, or for things they might have done abroad, like joining leftist student groups, and would receive lengthy jail sentences. Kennedy resisted this idea, but he continued to support the shah.

In late 1961, the shah appointed Ali Amini as prime minister. Amini was a former Iranian ambassador to Washington. He had trained as an economist, and he had been working for the Iranian government since the 1940s. Like Qavam and Mossadeq before him, Amini was a visionary that seemed to at last offer Iran the chance to evolve into a liberal democracy. He was a natural reformer, and he prepared a far-reaching plan to both modernize and liberalize Iran's government. In fact, it was under his leadership that the first steps toward land reform were taken. Unfortunately, his time in office was to be brief. Amini could never overcome the fact that he lacked the broad support that Mossadeq had enjoyed. More importantly, the shah neither liked nor trusted him. This was probably due to the fact that he was both popular and effective—he was a threat to the shah's rule and to his increasingly irrational belief that he was the only true leader of the country. In July 1962, just a few months after the shah's visit to Washington, the two men faced off over military spending. As an economist, Amini knew that the country was on the verge of a financial collapse and that the money earmarked for the army should be limited. But the shah would not hear of it, and Amini was out.

In the summer of 1962, Mohammed Reza announced his White Revolution ("white" because presumably no blood was to be shed). It was widely applauded in the West, where it was seen as a sign that the shah was finally willing to solve some of his country's most pressing problems. The revolution consisted of six major points: the sale of certain state-owned industries to provide money for farmers, the nationalization of forests (meaning that the state would control the timber industry), profit-sharing for workers in certain jobs (they would earn extra money if their businesses made money), the formation of a Literacy Corps, the revision of voting laws (which greatly increased the rights of women), and land reform.

Land reform was particularly important to many Iranians because the wealthy and the clergy owned vast tracts of property, which impoverished peasants worked for very little money. The shah had given away some of the land his father had seized, and in 1962 and again in 1963, religious leaders encouraged riots in the cities of Qom and Tehran. These were violently suppressed, but they were yet another indication that the shah was out of touch with the still-powerful clerics.

Despite the shah's failures on some fronts, many of his attempts at modernization were successful. Women enjoyed more freedom in Iran than almost anywhere else in the region, and the literacy rate increased dramatically. The West began to view the shah as a great reformer and a symbol of what could be achieved elsewhere in the world. He was considered, somewhat condescendingly, a benevolent dictator, a liberal foe of conservative religious leaders. The power of the Islamic clerics was not taken seriously by either the shah or his Western allies. They seemed to believe that once people were exposed to the promise of material goods and personal freedoms that Westerners enjoyed, they would abandon the mullahs and ayatollahs. The type of religious conviction advocated by the clerics was labeled "fanaticism," and it was on its way out. Or so the shah and his allies thought.

An elderly woman in a small village is shown teaching children to read.

In the meantime, the shah continued to travel the world, socializing and playing politics. He sided with Israel in the Six-Day War of 1967, to the shock and horror of his Arab neighbors, who were all intent on ridding the region of the Jewish state. While his decision earned the praise of the United States and the West, which supported Israel's right to exist, it infuriated the Arab world and the Muslim clerics in Iran. But the shah was more worried about pleasing the West. He was still obsessed with building a vast army, and he maintained his personal fascination with weaponry. The closer he allied himself to the West, the more arms they sold him.

Throughout the 1960s, Mohammed Reza continued to spend money on his military. Both President Kennedy and his successor, Lyndon Johnson, worried openly about the shah's ability to lead his country. He was still being described in an American intelligence report as "weak-willed" and "erratic," undesirable traits in an ally. Both leaders feared that the shah was out of touch with his people, that he was too quick to use violence to suppress opposition to his rule, and that his desire to build his army stemmed from his own obsession with weapons. Still, the shah was one of the only leaders in the region who was friendly to the West. Arab nationalism had been on the rise since World War II, and by the 1960s it was in full force. Arab nations that had been ruled by Western powers had seen the profits from their natural resources, primarily oil, enrich foreign powers while their own people remained poor. In response to the perception that the West continued to rule the Middle East, many Arab leaders were demanding to control their own oil fields and finding an ally in Russia. Iran remained allied with the West, and that, for a time, would be the shah's salvation.

Ayatollah Khomeini bitterly opposed the shah. Khomeini was openly critical of the shah's efforts to impose Western culture on Iran.

6

Nemesis:
Ayatollah Ruhollah
Khomeini

The biography of Shah Mohammed Reza Pahlavi would be incomplete without a discussion of the man who was to become his greatest and most determined nemesis, Ayatollah Ruhollah Khomeini. The ayatollah's life story is essentially the opposite of Mohammed Reza's, and Khomeini's rise to power clearly reflects the shah's inability to recognize the dissatisfaction of his people. While the West was flattering the shah, Iranians were protesting in the streets. And while Khomeini's status as the savior of Iran grew, so did the shah's image as an oppressive figurehead.

Khomeini was the leading ayatollah (supreme religious leader) of Iran's Shi'ites. His goal was to establish in Iran an Islamic republic, a government based on the religious laws of Islam and run by Islamic clergy. He was the man most directly responsible for the shah's fall—with the possible exception of the shah himself.

Khomeini was not the first religious leader to speak out against the shah. The list of Mohammed Reza's critics was long and diverse, and included both Muslim clerics and secular leaders who accused him of a host of crimes—from human rights abuses to corruption. In many respects, the shah's detractors had valid points. His secret police, SAVAK, were considered brutal and unjust by human rights groups worldwide. The shah's large extended family was extraordinarily wealthy, and much of its money came from land and industries that had been seized by the shah's father or developed under the shah using public money. There is also substantial evidence to suggest that they were corrupt—they skimmed money from public projects, took kickbacks from contractors, and profited from nationalized industries.

If the shah had been more open to the complaints of his critics, the events of the late 1970s might never have occurred. But he would not tolerate such dissedent about himself or his family; he believed that he was the divinely chosen embodiment of Iran. In his opinion, he knew what was best for the nation and those who challenged him were simply to be silenced. His own advisers were too afraid to tell him the truth about his reputation, and so he pressed forward, all the while drawing more and more hatred from a populace that he was convinced loved him.

Khomeini, on the other hand, was naturally charismatic and comfortable interacting with the "common" people, whom the shah avoided. Although his early history is a bit unclear, Khomeini was probably born on November 2, 1902, in the small city of Khomeini, from which he later took his name. He was the fourth child of Sayyad Mostafa Musavi, a poor religious scholar. His name, Ruhollah, means "the spirit of God." His father died in 1903, and young Ruhollah was sent to live with an aunt, who was wealthy compared to his family. His aunt sent him to Islamic schools, where he studied the Koran, the Muslim bible, and learned to read and write. The school stressed leading a religious life, and Khomeini was drawn to the lessons of the Koran. When he was in his late teens, he moved to the city of Qom, in north-western Iran, to complete his studies. Qom was the center of conservative religious teaching, and Khomeini was taught by some of the greatest Shi'ite scholars in Iran.

Like his father, Khomeini chose a spiritual life. Most of his time was spent reading and reciting from the Koran and discussing his readings with other students and scholars. He was a bright and ambitious student. By the time he had reached his mid-20s, he had become a mullah, a Shi'ite priest. He would lecture on ethics and philosophy, and word spread that he was a passionate and inspirational leader. He began to attract more and more students.

As part of Mohammed Reza's plan to westernize Iran, he took steps to do away with the traditions of Islam, which he felt were holding the country back. As discussed in earlier chapters, his reforms were embraced by some and regarded as anti-Islamic by others. To Khomeini, the shah was not only changing the country for the worse, he was directly insulting Allah, a sin punishable by death. As the shah ordered the abandonment of the Islamic calendar and adoption of the Western one, and the banning of such fundamental Islamic traditions as beards and turbans for men and veils for women, religious leaders became increasingly more vocal about their wish to break free of his reign. Khomeini was among them. Mohammed Reza wanted to limit the power of the mullahs and ayatollahs, so he began placing many of them under house arrest. This meant that they could not go to mosques or marketplaces, which made it difficult for them to spread their message of rebellion.

In 1930 Khomeini had married Batul bin Mirza Muhammad al-Saqafi, the 10-year-old daughter of a fellow religious leader. Throughout the 1930s and 1940s, he traveled the country lecturing to students. He drew large crowds wherever he spoke, and he wrote extensively about Islamic law. His work helped him rise through the ranks of the Shi'ite clergy, and sometime in the mid-1950s he was made an ayatollah. An ayatollah is a Shiite religious leader that has the ability to rule on religious law. In other words, the Shi'ite clergy had made him a sort of judge, one with absolute power to interpret Islamic law. If there is a conflict in the community, or if someone is accused of violating Islamic law, an ayatollah can settle the issue or punish the individual. It is a position of tremendous respect and power among religious Shi'ites. By the time Khomeini was named ayatollah, he already had a large following of disciples. His new position only served to make him more popular, especially among young men unhappy with the shah's reforms.

He first came to the attention of the world in 1963 when he helped organize anti-land reform riots in Qom. He believed that the shah was trying to weaken Islamic leadership by taking away land owned by Muslim clerics. Though it would later appear that he opposed all of the shah's reforms, at the time, he was not against giving women the right to vote, or the nationalization of certain industries. The issues that were critical to him were his perception that the shah was a dictator, that he had made Iran subservient to the West, and that he supported Israel's right to exist. Khomeini, like many other Muslim clerics, believed that the existence of a Jewish state among Muslim countries was an affront to their religion. The clerics thought that by supporting Israel and its great ally, the United States, the shah was insulting Islam. In his speech, he criticized the shah for making Islam less of a force in Iran. He was immediately arrested, and his followers rioted in the streets of Qom and several other cities. Eager to stop the violence, the shah released Khomeini.

Now Khomeini was not only a powerful cleric, but he was also the most prominent critic of the shah. Mohammed Reza realized that Khomeini was a threat to his control of the country, but he was afraid to arrest him again. It was not good for Iran's image in the West to have students violently demonstrating against him. At the same time, it was dangerous to allow Khomeini to stir up anti-shah sentiment with every speech he gave. So, in 1964, under pressure from the government, Khomeini was forced to flee Iran. He realized that eventually the shah would arrest him and that he would be stronger without the shah's police monitoring his every move. He was right, and even after he settled in neighboring Iraq, he was still considered to be the ultimate spiritual leader by many of Iran's Shi'ites. His visitors were watched by Iraqi and Iranian secret police, but he was still able to smuggle his speeches and writings to his followers in Iran. His exile made him a martyr to his followers and to others, and his popularity continued to grow.

In October 1978 Iraq exiled Khomeini at a show of support for Iran. He moved to France, where he broadcast radio speeches calling for the shah's overthrow and imprisonment for crimes against Allah. When the shah left Iran for the last time in 1979, Khomeini took control. The ayatollah's return was celebrated by tens of thousands of people singing in the streets. He would be as bloody and ruthless in his rule of Iran as he had accused the shah of being, and he slaughtered those he felt had supported the shah. He also went after people who did not adhere to his version of Shi'ite law, and women, in particular, lost many of the rights they had enjoyed under the shah. Among other things, women could be beaten for appearing in public without a veil covering most of their face.

Khomeini would lead Iran through the American embassy hostage crisis (see chapter 10) and through the Iran-Iraq War. In September 1980, in a dispute over territory, Iraq had invaded Iran. Because the seizure of the U.S. Embassy had been a violation of international law, many countries refused

Even in exile, the ayatollah continued to attract followers. Supporters eagerly greeted Ayatollah Khomeini when he returned from exile in 1979.

to help Iran. The Iraqis were successful at the beginning, but by 1982 the Iranians had forced them to retreat. Khomeini said Iran would not stop fighting until the Iraqi president, Saddam Hussein, was out of office. He believed that Hussein held Iraq back from being a true, religious, Islamic nation. The war brought a new set of horrors to an already devastated Iran, for example, the Iraqis bombed Iranian cities and used poison gas on their troops. Cut off from the world and running out of the supplies it needed to continue the war, Iran was forced to accept a United Nations cease-fire agreement in 1988.

The last years of Khomeini's reign were marked by problems. The eight-year war destroyed Iran's economy, and many of Khomeini's fellow clergy in the government fought among themselves. One of Khomeini's last official acts was to sentence the English novelist Salman Rushdie to death for writing *The Satanic Verses,* which Khomeini believed was offensive to Islam. When Khomeini died in Tehran on June 3, 1989, millions in Iran mourned his death; but his death paved the way for an easing of strict religious law.

The wealthy shah lived in sharp contrast to the people he ruled. Mohammed Reza sought absolute power over Iran and its people, and crushed his opposition through imprisonment, torture, and executions.

7

Pride Before the Fall

After 1962, Shah Mohammed Reza Pahlavi's rule became more and more despotic. As he told President Kennedy, he was bent on controlling Iran, even if it meant violating human rights by imprisoning, torturing, and even killing his political opponents. He was increasingly assured that he was the physical representation of the spirit of the Iranian people: He was the state.

But Mohammed Reza was full of contradictions. He was a tyrannical ruler who crushed his opposition without mercy, personally making sure that those who spoke out against him were sent to jail and, sometimes, to their death. But he was growing more and more insecure about his hold on power and about the love of his people. His advisers were afraid to oppose him, and increasingly he fell under the influence of his sister, Ashraf. While his advisers could be fired or imprisoned for objecting to any of the shah's whims, his sister remained a dominant force in his life. He respected her advice, and she had a much stronger personality than he did. She was also more corrupt, and she took advantage of her position within the regime. While all of the Pahlavis grew wealthy in the late 1960s and early 1970s, no one was quite as obvious about it as Ashraf. If public money was to be spent on construction in Tehran, for example, Ashraf would either assign the work to a company that she or a relative owned, or she would demand enormous payoffs in return for the contract to do the work. While his supporters claimed that it was arguable whether or not the shah was entirely aware of his family's behavior, he certainly benefited from it. By the early 1970s, he was one of the wealthiest men in the world.

He also now had an heir, Crown Prince Reza, born in 1960. The prince was followed by two sisters, Farahnaz and Leila, and another son, Ali Reza. Queen Farah had proven to be a major asset to the shah. Not only had she given birth to sons, but she was beloved by the Iranian people. Unlike her husband, she was naturally warm and friendly, and she made an effort to reach out to "common" people—something her husband was never comfortable doing. While her husband allotted funds for schools and hospitals to be built, Farah was the one who actually went out and visited them. By most accounts, they had a happy marriage, though the shah was openly unfaithful to her. Ashraf disliked Farah because Farah threatened Ashraf's influence over the shah, but the queen was too well liked to be done away with. Farah pushed her husband to extend women's rights, and by the 1970s women in Iran had more freedom than almost anywhere else in the Middle East. Farah's one flaw was something that was beyond her control— she was Western. She had been schooled in Europe, she traveled frequently, and she wore Western-style clothing and hairstyles (all of the women in the royal family did). When the revolution arrived, this would be held up as an example of the shah's betrayal of Iran's traditions.

Before the revolution, the two enjoyed a whirlwind life. Even during the early days of the White Revolution, when his position had been at its most precarious, the shah had been a figure on the world's social scene. He invited film stars and moguls to his beach resort, and he spent winters skiing in Switzerland. He seemed either unaware or unmoved by the fact that while progress was being made, most Iranians still lived as peasants.

As the shah continued to be flattered by his advisers and courted by the heads of Western countries, his ego and his ambition grew. Khomeini continued to be a thorn in his side, but the shah was convinced that Khomeini's power was fleeting and that he could easily be done away with. After Amini, no prime minister had the courage or the independence to challenge him openly. He promoted prime ministers who would bend easily to his will. Asadollah Alam, who served from 1962 to 1964, was a close friend, and presided over the brutal repression of opposition to the White Revolution. He allowed the shah to distance himself from the carnage. His successor, Hasan Ali Mansur, was assassinated in January 1965. Mansur was followed by Amir Abbas Hoveyda, who would serve until the revolution, when he was arrested on the orders of Ayatollah Khomeini and executed for treason.

The 1960s were a time of reform coupled with repression. But 1971 would prove to be one of the most important years of the shah's reign. Not only did it mark the 30th anniversary of his rule, and nearly the 10th anniversary of the White Revolution, but the shah chose to recognize it as the 2500th anniversary of the rule of Cyrus the Great (even though it was not quite that many years), the first true leader of the civilization that had become Iran. This year also marked the first time the Organization of Petroleum Exporting Countries (OPEC) flexed its muscles.

OPEC was and is a major force in the world economy. It was founded by countries whose oil industries were at one time

The Shahyad Monument in Tehran was built to honor several anniversaries in Iran, including the rule of Cyrus the Great in ancient Persia.

dominated by Western powers. Now, they banded together to control the international price of oil. By agreeing to work as a team, they could decide how much a barrel of oil was worth. Because they controlled the majority of the world's oil supply, they could set high prices without worrying that another country would steal away their buyers with lower prices. In the early 1970s, OPEC held the West "hostage." For example, when OPEC decided on a major price increase in 1979, the United States went through a gasoline shortage so severe that the government instituted odd and even days for buying gas. If a license plate had an even number, the car owner could purchase gas on one day; if it was odd, the owner had to wait until the next day. The shah was a leading proponent of OPEC, and in 1971 he let the West know he was serious by pushing the first of the group's price increases. Not only did it allow him to get the upper hand in dealing with his allies, it made him and his family a fortune.

He put this wealth on display for the world with his celebration of Cyrus's regime. He threw a massive party at Persepolis, the site of one of the great cities of Iran's past. He invited world leaders, celebrities, and royalty to join him on October 15th, for what the palace described as an "assembly [that] will make Persepolis the center of gravity of the world." He built a massive tent city to accommodate his guests and flew in chefs from Paris to cook for them. President Richard Nixon sent his vice president, Spiro Agnew, and nine kings were on hand. The entire event cost an estimated $300 million. At the time, the average income in Iran was $500 a year. The people of Iran stood by and watched a party that they were not allowed to attend and that cost their government millions of dollars.

With the Persepolis party, Mohammed Reza drew the eyes of the world to Iran. Certainly, life had improved in many ways under his regime. Still, liberal journalists and politicians in the West, even those that could acknowledge his good deeds, began to openly criticize the shah's excesses. It was true that there were new hospitals and schools, and more Iranians than ever were literate, but SAVAK monitored every aspect of daily life. Even a suspicion of dissent was enough to get a person arrested. The shah seemed more out of touch with the problems of his nation than ever.

The next few years would bring unprecedented wealth to Iran, which had finally nationalized the oil industry completely in the 1960s. Iran was viewed as the police force of the Middle East, and the shah's relationship with President Nixon was strong. Nixon's secretary of state, Henry Kissinger, had pushed an agreement that allowed the shah to purchase whatever arms he wanted from the United States (only nuclear weapons were off limits) as a payoff for the shah's loyalty.

In the early 1970s the United States was still embroiled in the Vietnam War, a war that was essentially being fought to keep Communists out of power in Southeast Asia. America hoped to avoid having to send troops to the Middle East. With the shah in power, the United States could be assured that Communists would not take control. That was of utmost importance, especially now that oil was at stake. The shah took advantage of his position and went on a massive military spending spree. He boasted that by the year 2000, Iran would be a power of world class, economically and militarily second to none except the United States and the Soviet Union.

The reality was far different. His people were furious, and with good reason. The economy, despite the boost from oil revenues, was out of control. Inflation, which is when the price of goods rises faster than the per capita income, was rampant. Peasants flooded the cities in search of work, only to find their situation was no better than it had been in their villages. The country's agricultural industry had been essentially abandoned as money was poured into oil exploration, but many of the high paying jobs in the oil business were given to foreigners, who lived in glittering, guarded enclaves. Iranians grew increasingly hostile to foreign powers, particularly America, which they regarded as responsible for the shah's rule. Since the overthrow of Mossadeq, the shah was seen as answering to the United States—in other words he had become an American puppet. Public services like hospitals and schools fell into disrepair as the shah ignored the needs of his people in the interest of building his military. Worst of all, he was still ignoring the Muslim clerics, who had grown increasingly belligerent in their denouncements of him. The shah considered them both backward and powerless, but he was wrong. In fact, they were preaching to an audience of people that were desperate for someone, anyone, to offer them relief.

The shah, still isolated in his palace, refused to admit that storm clouds were gathering on the horizon, and his advisers were too afraid to tell him. In 1971, as he stood on a stage at Persepolis in front of a crowd of some of the most powerful people in the world, he could not know that within eight years he would be in exile from the country he believed he was destined to rule.

The shah is pictured in 1975 with his children, Princess Leila and Prince Ali Reza.

8

The
Revolution
Begins

S hah Mohammed Reza Pahlavi was not an easy man to define. While he was enjoying the life of the rich and famous, he often worried about money. He built a lavish vacation home on the Caspian Sea, and he would fly his private helicopter low over the waves so that his guests could leap out into the water. He and his wife had their official portraits painted by American Pop artist Andy Warhol, and they flew chefs in from Paris to cook for their dinner parties, yet he insisted that Iran's culture was superior to that of the West.

Though he had given Iranian women more rights than they had ever enjoyed before, in 1973 he told the Italian journalist Oriana Fallaci, "[Women have] never produced a Michelangelo or a Bach. You've never even produced a great cook. And don't talk of opportunities. Are you joking? Have you lacked the opportunity to give history a great cook? You have produced nothing great, nothing!"

Despite all of his flaws, and despite the rumblings of unhappiness from his people, the United States still endorsed him. He was an important world leader. It had agreed to continue supplying him with arms, and in 1976, President Jimmy Carter began negotiations to sell him nuclear reactors. Iran was the most modern country in the Middle East, and Mohammed Reza believed that it was on the brink of becoming a superpower. Yes, some of his people had suffered, but the prosperity and respect Iran now enjoyed made all of that worthwhile. Or so he thought.

The average Iranian disagreed. In 1970 the Shah's sister, who was Iran's delegate to the United Nations, became the head of the U.N. Human Rights Commission. At the same time, SAVAK was becoming known worldwide for its brutality and injustice. By the mid-1970s, Ayatollah Khomeini's status was on the rise among both Iranians and human rights activists, while the shah's status continued to erode. He had grown from a timid, indecisive ruler into a tyrant that threw his opponents in jail. He was so out of touch that even his wife, the Empress Farah, could not seem to get through to him. When she pointed out that Iranians were unhappy with his rule, he would tell her she made too much of things, and that "My people love me. I am Iran."

The corruption of his friends and family didn't help matters. Iran was now a divided nation: the upper classes profited from the shah's dealings with the West, while the middle and lower classes struggled with the changes to their society. A 1976 CIA report describes Princess Ashraf as having, "a near legendary reputation for financial corruption." The people of Iran, on the other hand, were little or no better off financially than they had been before the White Revolution. Their religious and political leaders had been dragged off to jail, and some had been executed or exiled. Their sons were forced to enlist in the shah's army. But there was hope. Broadcasting his message from Iraq, and then from France, the Ayatollah Khomeini told the people that Islam offered the key to happiness. Iran needed to be liberated from the evils of the West, of the shah, and return to its Islamic roots, and he would help to lead them. To a people that had suffered for generations, the message was impossible to resist.

One of the first signs that the breaking point had been reached was the outward display of anti-American sentiment. Since the overthrow of Mossadeq, it was commonly believed by Iranians that the shah was being propped up by the United States. Clearly, there was some truth to this, since without the help of the CIA, the shah probably would have lost his throne in 1953. The Americans wanted stability in the region for strategic and financial reasons—they wanted to protect their oil supply and prevent the spread of Communism—and the shah was their most reliable ally in the Middle East. President Richard Nixon and his secretary of state, Henry Kissinger, both considered the shah a close friend. Still, the United States was generally regarded as being less imposing than Britain or Russia, and even middle-class Iranians often sent their children to study in America. But by the 1970s, anti-American sentiment was rampant, even in big cities like Tehran. Iranians resented the U.S. influence on its policies over things like the recognition of Israel and the repression of Communism, and that resentment had boiled over into hatred. The stated goal of young revolutionaries was the institution of a new, Islamic government that would not answer to the West. America's involvement with the shah was about to become a major flashpoint in the swift, decisive battle for Iran.

In 1977 Iran was an unstable country that was ready for revolution. Mohammed Reza refused to listen to the few advisers that dared tell him that his status as king was at risk. The Iranian economy, which had boomed in the early 1970s because of oil exports, began to collapse in 1975. Imported goods were being sold at prices that were subsidized by the

These men protest against the shah over the degeneration of state affairs in Iran. Many Iranians saw the shah as nothing more than an American puppet.

government as part of its trade deals with Western countries. Iranian farmers and manufacturers could not match these artificially low prices and still make a profit, so the gap between rich and poor continued to widen. Peasants that could no longer survive by working their land flooded into urban centers where, as in the years before the White Revolution, they found little work and crowded conditions. Rather than train these workers, foreign businesses and even Iran's own industries brought in skilled laborers from abroad.

The shah seemed unable to comprehend the seriousness of his country's condition. For example, between 1973 and 1977, inflation had spiraled out of control. Instead of instituting economic policies that might have helped the situation, the shah decided to concentrate on imprisoning price gougers, people who charged far more for a product than it is really worth. It was a strange tactic—price gouging is common during times of inflation, but it is not really the cause of inflation. But the shah believed he could make an example of these petty criminals, and he sent a special squad of investigators into the bazaars, or markets, to hunt down traders that were charging too much for their goods. The agents imprisoned hundreds of people, many of whom were highly respected. The bazaar was not just a place to shop in Iran, it was the heart of a community. The campaign did nothing to prevent inflation, but it served as yet another example of the shah's ineptitude.

Meanwhile, Islam was experiencing a major revival in 1977. Young people had been drawn to religious schools in increasing numbers since the 1960s, and they had become hotbeds of political dissent. Students in high schools and colleges with no religious affiliation began to talk more openly about Islam. It was a form of rebellion against the system, and it appealed to young Iranians who saw a bleak future for themselves under the shah. Women even began wearing the long black chador, a cape that covers everything but the eyes and mouth, to make a political statement. They were a symbol of a time when mullahs and ayatollahs dominated daily life, and they had been banned for a time by the shah. Their reappearance signaled a renewed devotion to Islam.

Then on October 9, 1977, two dozen masked students at Tehran University burned buses and smashed windows to protest the presence of women on campus. In traditional Islam, men and women cannot be schooled together. In the following weeks, several religious demonstrations sprang up in Qom, the conservative city in northwest Iran where Ayatollah Khomeini had taught before he was exiled. It may seem strange that young Iranians were asking for a return to traditional ways and that they were urging laws that would limit their personal freedoms. But they believed that the shah's desire to befriend the West and embrace its ways had led Iran astray. Islam offered an alternative to the shah.

The shah could not fathom why his people were turning to religion. To him, it was a step backward, and he continued to believe that his people would eventually thank him for his tough leadership. Yes, some had suffered, but it was for the greater good of Iran. Still, he was not completely immune to their complaints, especially since the new American president, Jimmy Carter, was so concerned with human rights. The shah announced a "liberalization" program, called *musharikat*. It was supposed to allow for greater political freedoms, but it was primarily for show. The shah wanted to appease the United States, Iranians said, so that he could continue to buy arms from them. He had done it with his White Revolution, they said, and now he was doing it again.

Mohammed Reza could claim he was liberalizing his regime, but SAVAK was still rounding up the opposition. In 1978, Ayatollah Khomeini's followers in Iran began distributing millions of dollars to the people of Iran. Much of the money had been raised by sympathetic Muslims in other countries. It was a bid to win supporters, and it worked. But the final straw came on January 8, 1978, when the shah's police opened fire on a crowd of Khomeini's supporters, killing at least two dozen of them. Black Friday, as it would be called, marked yet another decisive moment in the shah's collapse. Even those Iranians who had previously been undecided were enraged by the police brutality and by the shah's silence on the incident. In the next year there would be monthly demonstrations, followed by police clashes, and an estimated 10,000 to 12,000 protesters would be killed.

America continued to support the shah, even after these incidents and others. And the shah continued to believe that he was untouchable as long as the Americans supported him— and why would they not support him? He had been a strong ally; he had given them all that they had asked for and more. And the shah was not unlikable. His defenders said he was simply shy and unsure of himself and that his most dictatorial policies were simply his way of covering his shortcomings. Of course, his enemies viewed him as a spineless puppet that was easily swayed by the flattery of the West, particularly America. Certainly, while he believed he had been divinely chosen to lead Iran, he also lived in the shadow of his father's legacy. His father had abandoned the throne rather than answer to anyone, and the shah lacked his strength of character. As one European diplomat put it, "No one dared to conceal the truth from [the shah's] father. No one dared to tell the truth to the Shah."

In 1979 demonstrations against the monarchy and in support of
Khomeini were sweeping Iran.

9

Final Days

The curtain was beginning to descend on the reign of Shah Mohammed Reza Pahlavi. As his police and his army continued to clash with rioters, the United States began to rethink its position. First, both the Americans and the Soviets had a vested interest in maintaining good relations with the government of Iran. If there was to be a new power in place, they wanted it to be friendly. The new government was unlikely to forgive the United States if it continued to support Mohammed Reza in the face of massive protest. Second, the Americans and Soviets wanted to steer clear of one another. If the United States sent in troops to support the shah, the Soviets would feel compelled to intervene, since Iran shared its border. There were rumors that the Soviets supported the opposition, but it is more likely that they simply wanted the impending revolution to be over as quickly as possible. They did not want militant Islamic sentiment spreading to their own Muslim provinces.

So, Mohammed Reza found himself virtually alone. By January 1979, even his mother had fled the country as violence swept through cities and small towns all over Iran. Publicly, President Carter supported the shah, but privately he called the shah and encouraged him to give up the throne. The shah was forced to begin seriously considering abdication. He feared dying abroad, away from his home, the way his own father had. And the shah was feeling his mortality.

The shah had been receiving secret treatments for cancer of the lymph nodes since 1974. His supporters later argued that had he gone public with his disease, he might have been easily cured. But the shah realized that if word got out that he was sick, his opponents would view him as weak and step up their attacks on him. Only his wife, his personal physician, and a cancer specialist that was flown in from Paris every few months, knew about his illness. The shah was sick, he was tired, and his options were beginning to look like they had run out.

But Mohammed Reza would not give up his home as easily as he had in the 1950s when he had fled to Italy. This time he made one last attempt to stay in power. In January 1979, he picked a thin, nervous lawyer named Shahpur Bakhtiar, to head a new civilian government. He was the second in command of the National Front, one of the political parties the shah had set up during the White Revolution. It had become the moderate voice amid the din of revolution, a sort of link between the shah and Khomeini. Bakhtiar was considered a moderate, and was relatively pro-Western, and he seemed well-respected enough to keep his more religion oriented colleagues in check. Bakhtiar accepted the position but said that it remained to be seen what role Mohammed Reza would play. "We are not for a republic or a monarchy," he told an interviewer. "We are for a progressive democracy."

He even went so far as to offer that, "The Shah can remain in Iran if he gives us adequate guarantees of human rights." Unfortunately for the shah, Bakhtiar was quickly criticized by Karim Sanjabi, the head of the National Front, who insisted that "the only solution is that the Shah must go."

The shah's friends were now encouraging him to either flee or abdicate the throne to his 18-year-old son, Crown Prince Reza. The shah, at the urging of his sister, became convinced that if he left the country, things would settle down and either he or his son could return to the throne. He still believed that the majority of his people loved him, and he decided to use his illness as an excuse to leave. He would tell the world he was going abroad for a rest from his problems at home. But where would he go? The United States was reluctant to offer him refuge, in part because they were concerned for the safety of their citizens in Iran. In November 1978 an American oilman had been shot and killed by a crowd of protesters. Slogans such as "Death to Jimmy Carter" and "The Shah is a chained American dog" were common at rallies. Beyond that, the United States hoped to befriend the new government. The United States wanted to protect its interests and encourage the more moderate leaders of the opposition to take control. For the short term, the shah would visit his Arab neighbors, going first to Egypt and then to Morocco for what would be termed state visits.

Then, in late January 1979, a young university professor was shot dead while demonstrating against the shah. Ten thousand mourners, many of them middle-class men and women wearing Western-style suits and dresses, took to the streets of Tehran to mourn him. Tehran was under the control of a military governor named Gholam Ali Oveissi, and he gave permission for the march to take place and provided marchers with a squad of army rangers as protection. But as the crowd made its way into a square dedicated to the shah's father, it came head-to-head with army troops.

The nervous soldiers fired their machine guns over the heads of the marchers. The regular troops let loose a fusillade of automatic-rifle fire near the crowd to warn the marchers to halt. The colonel who was leading the rangers guarding the march came forward to stop the firing and was shot dead. The rangers retaliated, and the scene became a melee, as marchers ran for cover. At least five people were killed.

It was not the worst incident, but it was the final turning point for many middle-class Iranians. The result was chaos, army troops were harassed now at every turn. It was no longer just angry students and peasants throwing bricks and shouting for the shah's head—now educated, westernized men and women were joining in. One middle-aged architect, a graduate of the University of California in Los Angeles, told a *Newsweek* magazine reporter, "Until now, I have merely watched what has been going on. But now everything has gone too far. I felt I would be betraying my country by not joining these kids."

The shah was in a state of shock. He began summoning all of his advisers to the palace to ask them each the same question: "Where did it all go wrong?" He had never been interested in what his ministers thought, but now Mohammed Reza was desperately seeking advice and reassurance. A former cabinet minister, who had not been summoned to the palace for 27 years, was so shocked by the question that he was speechless. "It was very emotional," he said later. "The Shah did not seem to understand why the people of the country had turned against him."

The shah, now more isolated from his people than he had ever been before, was by turns angry and depressed. At times he seemed resigned to the notion that he would soon be forced to leave Tehran, but he was also positive that his flight would be short-lived. He truly believed that while he might never return to the throne, his son, Crown Prince Reza, would rule Iran as soon as the revolutionaries had been stopped.

An image of the shah was burned by angry protesters demonstrating outside the U.S. Embassy in Tehran in 1979.

For perhaps the first time in his life, Mohammed Reza was willing to admit that he had made mistakes. He acknowledged that SAVAK had been brutal, though he did not denounce his secret police outright. He seemed finally able to recognize the corruption of those close to him. The shah admitted that in his zeal to modernize and westernize Iran, he had ignored the needs of most Iranians. Still, he was convinced that the students who had taken to the streets to denounce him were Communists, and he could not understand why the West was not coming to his aid. "Very few of the youngsters parading behind Khomeini's picture had ever set foot in a mosque," he said. "Why can't the press see what Marx is doing behind Mohammed's banner?"

Despite his claims, the Carter Administration would not budge. It wanted the shah out of Iran because it hoped to maintain a friendly relationship with the country's new leadership—which by this time seemed inevitable. "If the U.S. doesn't care whether Iran becomes an Islamic republic and then one more [Communist] state, why should I take my country over the brink into civil war?" the shah demanded. But it was no use. He told Prime Minister Bakhtiar that he would leave Iran and agreed to stay on only long enough to confirm a new government. Money was no issue, since, by most estimates, he had put away at least $100 million in foreign banks. The United States had invited him to stay at the Palm Beach, Florida, estate of businessman Walter Annenberg until other arrangements could be made. He would not be flown to a major airforce base or given the welcome usually due a visiting dignitary. Instead, the Americans planned to usher the shah in quietly, so as not to draw attention to his presence. To the shah, it seemed a final indignity, but he no longer had a choice.

Mohammed Reza and Empress Farah spent their final days wandering the grounds of the palace. At one point, he picked up a handful of soil to take with him into exile. It was an emotional time for the shah, who had for so long believed that his destiny was to lead Iran to greatness. Instead, he found himself saying farewell to the people and places he had known his whole life. The only part of his beloved country left for him to cling to was a handful of dirt.

The day before he left, he called together the palace staff

and his bodyguards for a tearful goodbye. He met with his army commanders, who were still loyal to him. The shah's supporters say that he discouraged them from leading a coup against the new government, but his critics say he was more ambiguous. The truth is probably somewhere in between—he wanted to see the new regime destroyed, but he wanted no more blood on his hands. Finally, he and Farah hosted a dinner for the few close friends that still remained in Tehran. Their children were in school abroad, so on the morning of January 16, 1979, the shah and his wife departed for the airport with only their dogs, the court physician, and a bodyguard. As word spread throughout Tehran that their plane had left Iran for Egypt, there were spontaneous celebrations in the streets. Statues of the shah were toppled, drivers honked their horns and flashed their headlights, and people danced in the streets singing, "By the will of Khomeini, the Shah has fled. He shall not return!" The Pahlavi Dynasty had ended.

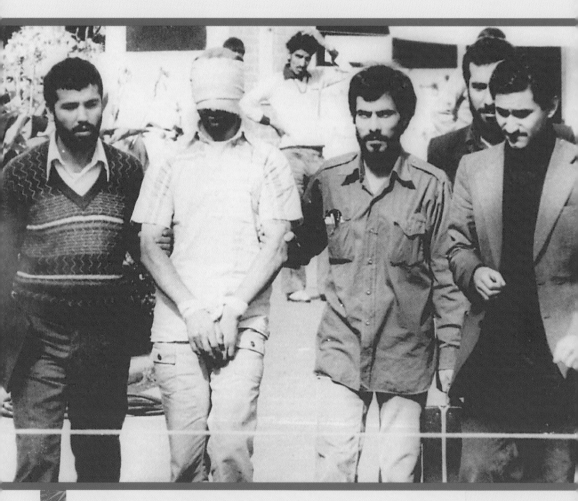

Militant Iranians flank one of the American hostages as he is led from the American embassy.

10

Hospitals and Hostages

S hah Mohammed Reza Pahlavi arrived in Egypt to the sort of red carpet reception reserved for heads of state. President Anwar Sadat, a friend of the shah's and a fellow believer in the secular modernization of the Middle East, welcomed the Pahlavis personally. The shah was still convinced that he would return to Iran, and his Egyptian hosts treated him accordingly. But in truth, Sadat knew that the chances of the shah's returning to power were slim. Sadat's own position was tenuous, as conservative Muslim activists were pressing for his removal from office. Like the shah, he was considered by some Egyptians to be a puppet of the West—he had recently signed a peace treaty with Israel, for example. Sadat would win the Nobel Peace Prize only to be assassinated by militants within the next few years. While he supported the shah, there was little he could do to help him. He could not offer the shah permanent residency because his people would not stand for it.

The shah had planned to spend only a few days in Egypt before heading to the United States, but King Hassan II of Morocco had invited him to visit on his way west. Hassan had been a supporter of the shah, a fellow monarch, and he clearly wanted to show solidarity. But when the shah arrived, Hassan kept his arrival low-profile. There were no Middle East leaders, with the exception of Sadat, that wanted to be too closely linked to the shah and the revolution in Iran. The leaders did not want their own people getting ideas.

Meanwhile, on February 1, 1979, Khomeini made a triumphant arrival in Tehran. The Carter Administration told the new government's leaders that it would accept the outcome of the revolution and would not interfere. Bakhtiar was arrested, and he would be executed after a public, and many would say staged, trial. It was clear within a matter of weeks that whatever hope the shah had for returning to Iran, it would not happen any time soon.

Mohammed Reza would stay in Morocco for several weeks, during which time it became increasingly clear that Hassan wanted him to leave. Many suspected that the shah was lingering in the region in the hopes that he could soon return to his home. Events in Iran made it clear that was not to be. The revolution had been a complete success, and the country had been transformed overnight into an Islamic state ruled by an ayatollah. Hassan worried that his fellow Arabs, including his own subjects, would object to the shah's presence. Mohammed Reza become a pariah, even among his friends.

Those friends included the United States. On February 22, the shah told the American ambassador to Morocco that he was ready to move to the United States. But the Carter Administration had decided that the shah was no longer welcome. The presence of the shah would put the thousands of American businesspeople and diplomats still in Iran at risk. It was decided that while the shah would technically still be allowed in the country, the situation was simply too tense to let him come immediately. President Carter told an adviser that he did not want the shah playing tennis while Americans were being kidnapped or killed. The advisers started to look for a country that would take him.

The shah took the news with dignity, but he was adamant about being close to his family. He suggested Mexico—his mother was in California, and Ashraf had a home in New York City. Mexico turned him down. The shah had become a symbol of brutal dictatorship that no leader wanted to be associated with. Whether or not the shah was truly as bad as many believed no longer mattered. His rule had been despotic, SAVAK had become a byword for police brutality, and his personal wealth was proof of his regime's corruption. Only South Africa and Paraguay were willing to take him in.

Finally, the United States convinced the Bahamas to take the shah. Arguably, his money was a major incentive (his 10-week stay there would cost him $1.2 million), but either way, it was a good temporary solution. But his life there would not be easy. He had been condemned to death in absentia by the new Iranian government, as had his wife, his mother, and his sister. Yasir Arafat, the head of the Palestinian Liberation Organization, which fought for the Arab overthrow of Israel, had threatened to send assassins after the shah and his family. The children visited their parents but returned to school in the United States under heavy guard. Worst of all, the Bahamian government, not wanting trouble, forbade the shah to speak publicly about the situation in Iran, where mass executions were already underway. When Mohammed Reza learned that Amir Abbas Hoveyda had been executed, he said that he shut himself up for a day to pray. Perhaps he felt guilty, since he had had Hoveyda, a loyal minister to the end, arrested in 1978 in an attempt to appease the opposition. Under the intense strain, the shah's health worsened.

Mexico had finally agreed, under U.S. pressure, to admit the shah. But after a month in Mexico he needed treatment for his cancer that was not available there. Through several friends, including businessman David Rockefeller and former Secretary of State Henry Kissinger, he asked permission to seek medical care in New York City. Carter had little choice but to honor his request. The shah had been America's ally for 40 years, and many in Washington, particularly Republicans, thought his exile was shameful. What leader would trust America in the future, Kissinger publicly asked, when they saw that the payoff for friendship was abandonment?

The United States by this time had established a relationship with the new Iranian prime minister, Mehdi Bazargan. It was hoped that the reasonable Bazargan would keep Khomeini in check. Bazargan was progressive, though rigged elections in August 1979 had left his power shaky at best. Khomeini's hard-line Islamic fundamentalists had succeeded in establishing their version of a constitution, and things looked bleak for those who did not wholeheartedly embrace conservative Islam. When the Americans alerted Bazargan that the shah had cancer and was being admitted to the United States for treatment, not for permanent residency, Bazargan reluctantly gave his approval. In October 1979 the shah flew to New York City, where he checked into the Sloan-Kettering Cancer Institute.

Unfortunately, Bazargan was not strong enough to stop Khomeini's followers, who saw the shah's arrival in New York as a repeat of the 1953 U.S.-backed coup against Mossadeq. On November 4, 1979, hundreds of radical demonstrators breached the walls of the U.S Embassy in Tehran and took its 66 staff members hostage. Khomeini stunned the world by immediately applauding the takeover and calling its leaders heroes. It would be 444 days before the last 52 hostages (14 were released early) would be freed. In that time, they would suffer through meager rations of bread, cold rice, and cold soup. After 20 days, the hostages were bound, blindfolded, and moved from the embassy to a series of makeshift prisons. The American people blamed the shah, and then blamed Carter for allowing Mohammed Reza into the United States.

With his cancer treatment completed, it was time again for the shah to find a home. This time, Panama took him in, mostly because its leader, General Omar Torrijos, liked Carter. There would be an election in November 1980, and Torrijos was afraid a Republican would win. He had negotiated a treaty for control of the Panama Canal with Carter, and he wanted to see Carter stay in office. The shah's time in Panama was troublesome, though Torrijos was more lenient than the Bahamians. He called Mohammed Reza, "Señor Shah," and spoke to him often about his situation. Torrijos was essentially a dictator, too, but a beloved and benevolent figure with a dislike of monarchies. The shah still believed that his family was destined to rule Iran, and he refused to give up the hope that his son would someday lead the country. Torrijos once asked him if he was not, "aware that your people wanted a change?" The shah replied, "I was going to change. I was going to give them an alternative. I was going to leave my son." When Torrijos asked whether he had wanted to save the people or the monarchy, the shah had answered, "Saving the monarchy is saving the people." He still did not understand what had happened in Iran.

On March 23, 1980, with the shah in desperate need of surgery, he and his wife left for Egypt. The United States had been trying to negotiate for the release of the hostages, and the Panamanians had become involved as well. The shah said that he would be more comfortable among friends, and Sadat had invited him to Cairo for medical treatment. Egyptians rioted upon hearing the news. There was some talk that the shah's plane would be diverted, that he would be turned over to Iran and tried for crimes against the state. But he arrived in Egypt safely and was greeted by Sadat, who was shocked at his appearance. He was now gaunt and pale, and it was clear he did not have much time left.

The flag-draped coffin of Shah Mohammed Reza Pahlavi is surrounded by his family members and Egyptian President Anwar Sadat (center) in Egypt.

In Egypt, with his wife, children, and Ashraf at his side, he underwent the last of his cancer treatments. The family had suffered—Ashraf's son had been assassinated in Paris, and Farah was on the verge of physical and emotional collapse. His condition was grave, and it was clear soon after his arrival that the end was near. It was the cause of rejoicing in Iran, while Americans hoped that it would lead to the freeing of the hostages.

Shah Mohammed Reza Pahlavi died on the morning of June 27, 1980. In Iran, the announcement was met with joy. Radio Tehran stated, "Mohammed Reza Pahlavi, the bloodsucker of the century, has died at last." The official Iranian news agency compared him to Egyptian kings that had grown wealthy off the work of their subjects, and said, "The treacherous Shah lies next to the tomb of the ancient Egyptian pharaohs . . . in disgrace, misery and vagrancy." Sadat arranged a state funeral, at which the only Arab nation represented was Morocco. The shah's last request, according to Farah, had been that his body be returned to Iran, after the country's liberation from Khomeini, to be buried among his generals. To the end, the shah was sure that the Pahlavis were chosen by Allah to lead Iran to greatness. He also had said, "I commend the great Iranian people into the hands of the Crown Prince. God protect him. And this is my last wish."

During his rule, the shah focused on the build up of Iran's military forces. He hoped to make his army one of the most powerful in the world.

11

Mohammed Reza's Legacy

The United States marked Shah Mohammed Reza Pahlavi's death with a statement that noted only that he had been the leader of Iran for a lengthy period of time and that he had seen it through tremendous changes. Kissinger recalled him as a true American ally, and former president Richard Nixon noted that America's treatment of the shah in exile would be regarded as "one of the black pages of American history." Certainly, it has been the source of much debate. The shah was a poor ruler, but he was loyal to America, which had turned its back on him once he was no longer of use. The hostages were not freed until after Carter lost the election and Ronald Reagan was inaugurated. There are many that believe that if the Carter Administration had evacuated Americans from Iran instead of trying to appease Khomeini, the hostage crisis would never happened.

The hostages suffered much of the same inhumanity that the revolutionaries had accused the shah of allowing under SAVAK. They were interrogated, beaten, and degraded, and their only exercise was an hour of running in place each morning. Three months into their captivity, they were placed in small cells and denied access to one another. They were forced to stand before mock firing squads on several occasions. They were finally released on January 20, 1981, emaciated and traumatized by their ordeal.

The world had, for the most part, condemned the taking of the hostages. Iran's new leaders became pariahs. But they were inspirational to terrorists everywhere, who realized that the United States was not invulnerable. The Great Satan, as Khomeini called America, had weaknesses that could be exploited. The intense publicity the crisis received helped make Iran a focal point of world politics. Iran was a rogue nation of 33 million people, and it could no longer be ignored or treated as a pawn of larger countries.

Back in April 1979, Khomeini had declared Iran an Islamic Republic. The government led by Bazargan and his progressive supporters could not maintain control, and radical clerics grabbed power for themselves. A new constitution providing for an Islamic theocracy was ratified by popular referendum in December 1979. In elections in January 1980, Abolhassan Bani-Sadr, a moderate, was elected president. But later elections for the Majlis were won by the hard-line clerical Islamic Republican Party, which came to dominate Iran. But conflict between rival political groups continued, and by 1982 at least 4,500 people had been killed in political violence.

The Iran-Iraq War, mentioned earlier, led to further chaos until 1988, when Iran agreed to a United Nations brokered cease-fire. Khomeini died of a heart attack on June 3, 1989 and more than three million people attended his funeral. His handpicked spiritual successor was Ali Khamenei. Today, Iran is led by President Mohammed Khatami, a moderate that was elected in 1997. Power in Iran is split between young moderates that want to see a more free society and the conservative clergy that still want a conservative Islamic regime. The moderates scored a further triumph in the elections of February and May 2000. A moderate reformist coalition headed by Khatami won 189 out of 290 seats in the Majlis. Still, Islamic radicalism is a constant threat, and in 2002 American President George W. Bush labeled Iran part of an "axis of evil" in his first state of the union address.

The surviving Pahlavis continue to live comfortably in exile. The shah's sister, mother, and daughter Leila died. His son, Crown Prince Reza, continues to call for his reinstatement to the throne of Iran. Following the terrorist attacks on the United States on September 11, 2001, he has been getting more attention from the press. The shah's flaws are now often regarded as being the lesser of two evils when compared to the violence and support of terrorism of the Islamic regime that replaced him. Many Iranians that fled the country before and during the revolution still regard Mohammed Reza with great fondness and blame the United States for abandoning an ally when he needed help the most.

It is impossible to say what Iran might be like today had Shah Mohammed Reza Pahlavi continued to rule. Historians might never agree on Mohammed Reza—his reign was marked by achievements as well as significant failures. The brutality of his leadership was eventually equaled by the cruelty of the revolutionaries. In the end, the shah's story is a tragedy, both for his family and for his beloved country.

1919	Mohammed Reza Pahlavi is born on October 26th in Tehran, Iran.
1937	Mohammed Reza returns to Iran from school in Switzerland.
1939	Marries Princess Fawzia of Egypt.
1941	Reza Shah Pahlavi abdicates the throne of Iran; his son, Mohammed Reza Pahlavi, is crowned shah.
1944	Reza Shah dies in exile.
1948	Mohammed Reza and Princess Fawzia are divorced.
1949	Shah marries Soraya Esfandiari.
1950	Members of the Tudeh Party attempt to assassinate the shah; martial law is declared.
1951	Prime Minister Razmara is assassinated in February; many suspect the shah. In March, Mossadeq becomes prime minister.
1953	August 12, the shah dismisses Mossadeq and leaves the country. August 19, Mossadeq is overthrown, with the help of the CIA.
1958	Shah divorces Soraya because she has not produced an heir.
1959	Marries Farah Diba.
1962	President Kennedy meets with the shah and tells him to make reforms.
	In the summer, the shah announces the White Revolution reform project.
1963	Ayatollah Khomeini organizes a protest in Qom; riots break out, and Khomeini is arrested.
1972	Inflation in Iran begins to spiral out of control.
1977	Student riots break out in Tehran on October 9.
1978	American oilman is shot dead in Tehran in November.
1979	Shah flees Iran for Egypt in January, and eventually the United States.
	Khomeini returns to Iran in February from exile and becomes de facto leader. On November 4, Khomeini's followers overrun the American embassy in Tehran, taking its staff hostage.

1980   Shah dies of cancer in Egypt on June 27; Iranians celebrate the news of his death.

1981   American hostages are released on January 20.

1989   Ayatollah Khomeini dies on June 3.

Cockcroft, James D. *Mohammed Reza Pahlavi, Shah of Iran.* New York: Chelsea House, 1989.

Hoyt, Edwin Palmer. *The Shah: The Glittering Story of Iran and Its People.* P.S. Eriksson, 1976.

Sanghavi, Ramesa. *The Shah of Iran.* New York: Stein and Day, 1969.

Shawcross, William. *The Shah's Last Ride: The Fate of an Ally.* New York: Simon and Schuster, 1988.

Villiers, Gérard. *The Imperial Shah; An Informal Biography.* Boston, M.A.: Little, Brown, 1976.

Zabih, Sepehr. *The Mossadegh: Roots of the Iranian Revolution.* Chicago: Lake View Press, 1982.

Zonis, Marvin. *Majestic Failure: The Fall of the Shah.* Chicago: University of Chicago Press, 1991.

LINDA BARTH is a writer and editor living in Brooklyn, New York. She has a B.A. in history and English from Tufts University and an M.A. from the New York University School of Journalism. She has written for such magazines as *American Heritage* and *ym*, where she is currently an editor.

ARTHUR M. SCHLESINGER, jr. is the leading American historian of our time. He won the Pulitzer Prize for his book *The Age of Jackson* (1945) and again for a chronicle of the Kennedy Administration, *A Thousand Days* (1965), which also won the National Book Award. Professor Schlesinger is the Albert Schweitzer Professor of the Humanities at the City University of New York and has been involved in several other Chelsea House projects, including the series REVOLUTIONARY WAR LEADERS, COLONIAL LEADERS, and YOUR GOVERNMENT.